THE ROSARY HAS FIVE DECA[DES,] A DIFFERENT MYSTERY OF C[HRIST PER] DECADE. WHILE PRAYING A R[OSARY, CHOOSE ONE] OF FOUR SETS OF MYSTERIES TO FOCUS ON: THE JOYFUL, SORROWFUL, LUMINOUS, OR GLORIOUS MYSTERIES.

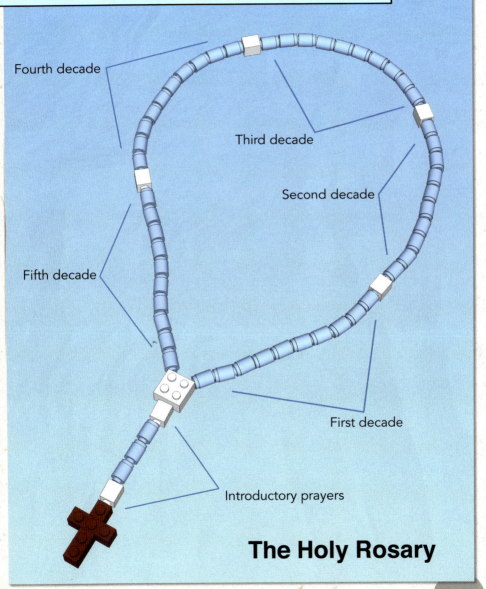

The Holy Rosary

THE THIRD JOYFUL MYSTERY IS THE NATIVITY.

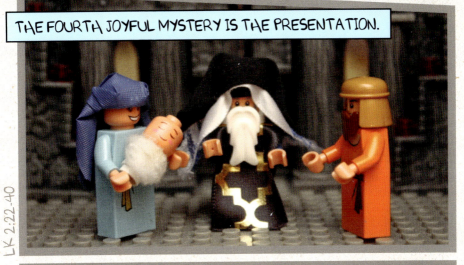

THE FOURTH JOYFUL MYSTERY IS THE PRESENTATION.

THE FIFTH JOYFUL MYSTERY IS THE FINDING OF JESUS IN THE TEMPLE.

THE **LUMINOUS MYSTERIES** CONTEMPLATE JESUS' PUBLIC LIFE AND MIRACLES.

THE FIRST LUMINOUS MYSTERY IS THE BAPTISM OF THE LORD.

THE SECOND LUMINOUS MYSTERY IS THE WEDDING AT CANA.

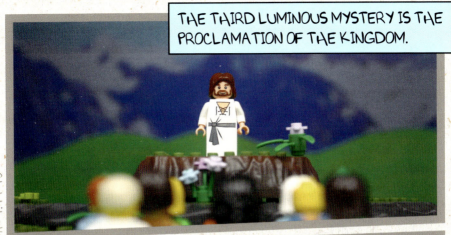

THE **SORROWFUL MYSTERIES** CONTEMPLATE THE SAD TIMES IN JESUS' LIFE.

THE FIRST SORROWFUL MYSTERY IS THE AGONY IN THE GARDEN.

THE SECOND SORROWFUL MYSTERY IS THE SCOURGING AT THE PILLAR.

THE THIRD GLORIOUS MYSTERY IS THE DESCENT OF THE HOLY SPIRIT.

ACTS 2:1,4

THE FOURTH GLORIOUS MYSTERY IS THE ASSUMPTION.

CCC 966

THE FIFTH GLORIOUS MYSTERY IS THE CORONATION.

REV 12:1

HERE'S HOW TO PRAY THE ROSARY.

1. In the name of the Father, and of the Son, and of the Holy Spirit. Amen.

I believe in God, the Father Almighty, creator of heaven and earth. I believe in Jesus Christ, His only Son, our Lord. He was conceived by the power of the Holy Spirit and born of the Virgin Mary. He suffered under Pontius Pilate, was crucified, died, and was buried. He descended into Hell. On the third day He rose again. He ascended into heaven and is seated at the right hand of the Father. He will come again to judge the living and the dead. I believe in the Holy Spirit, the holy catholic Church, the communion of saints, the forgiveness of sins, the resurrection of the body, and the life everlasting. Amen.

2. Our Father Who art in Heaven, hallowed be Thy Name; Thy kingdom come; Thy will be done on earth as it is in heaven. Give us this day our daily bread, and forgive us our trespasses, as we forgive those who trespass against us, and lead us not into temptation, but deliver us from evil. Amen.

3. Hail Mary, full of grace, the Lord is with thee. Blessed art thou amongst women, and blessed is the fruit of thy womb, Jesus. Holy Mary, Mother of God, pray for us sinners, now and at the hour of our death. Amen.

4. Glory be to the Father, and to the Son, and to the Holy Spirit, as it was in the beginning, is now, and ever shall be, world without end. Amen.

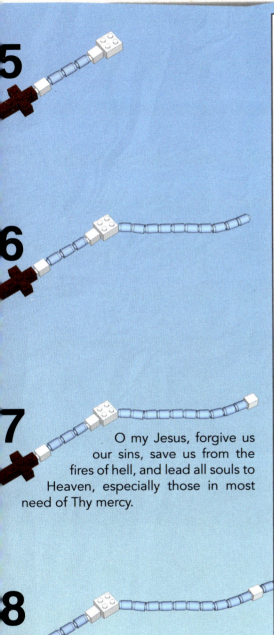

O my Jesus, forgive us our sins, save us from the fires of hell, and lead all souls to Heaven, especially those in most need of Thy mercy.

Rosary Instructions

Start by choosing which set of mysteries to meditate on.

Suggestions: Joyful on Monday and Saturday, Luminous on Thursday, Sorrowful on Tuesday and Friday, Glorious on Wednesday and Sunday.

1. Begin with the Sign of the Cross, followed by the Apostles' Creed prayer.

2. Pray one Our Father prayer, also called The Lord's Prayer.

3. Pray three Hail Mary prayers for the virtues of faith, hope, and charity.

4. Pray one Glory Be prayer.

5. State the first mystery, and pray one Our Father prayer.

6. Pray 10 Hail Mary prayers while contemplating the stated mystery.

7. Conclude the decade by praying the Glory Be prayer and the Fatima Prayer.

8. Continue saying four more decades, meditating on each of the five mysteries in order.

9. Conclude the decades by praying the Hail Holy Queen prayer.

10. Some people also recite the Rosary Prayer, the Memorare, and the Prayer to St. Michael the Archangel. Some also recite one Our Father prayer, one Hail Mary prayer, and one Glory Be prayer for the intentions of the pope.

11. Finally, conclude with the Sign of the Cross.

9 Hail, Holy Queen, mother of mercy, our life, our sweetness, and our hope. To thee do we cry, poor banished children of Eve. To thee do we send up our sighs, mourning and weeping in this valley of tears. Turn then, most gracious advocate, thine eyes of mercy toward us, and after this our exile show us the blessed fruit of thy womb, Jesus. O clement, O loving, O sweet Virgin Mary. Pray for us, O Holy Mother of God. That we may be made worthy of the promises of Christ.

> OKAY, CYNTHIA, LET'S OFFER THIS ROSARY FOR THE HOLY FATHER AND FOR HEALTH IN OUR FAMILIES.